THE TRUMP COLORING BOOK

LESLIE TRAN

The Trump Coloring Book

ISBN-13: 0-9978476-0-3
ISBN-10: 978-0-9978476-0-4

Give feedback on the book at:
Mr.LeslieTran@gmail.com

Join me on:
Twitter: @MrLeslieTran
Facebook: fb.com/MrLeslieTran
Tumblr: MrLeslieTran.tumblr.com
Instagram: instagram.com/MrLeslieTran

Printed in U.S.A

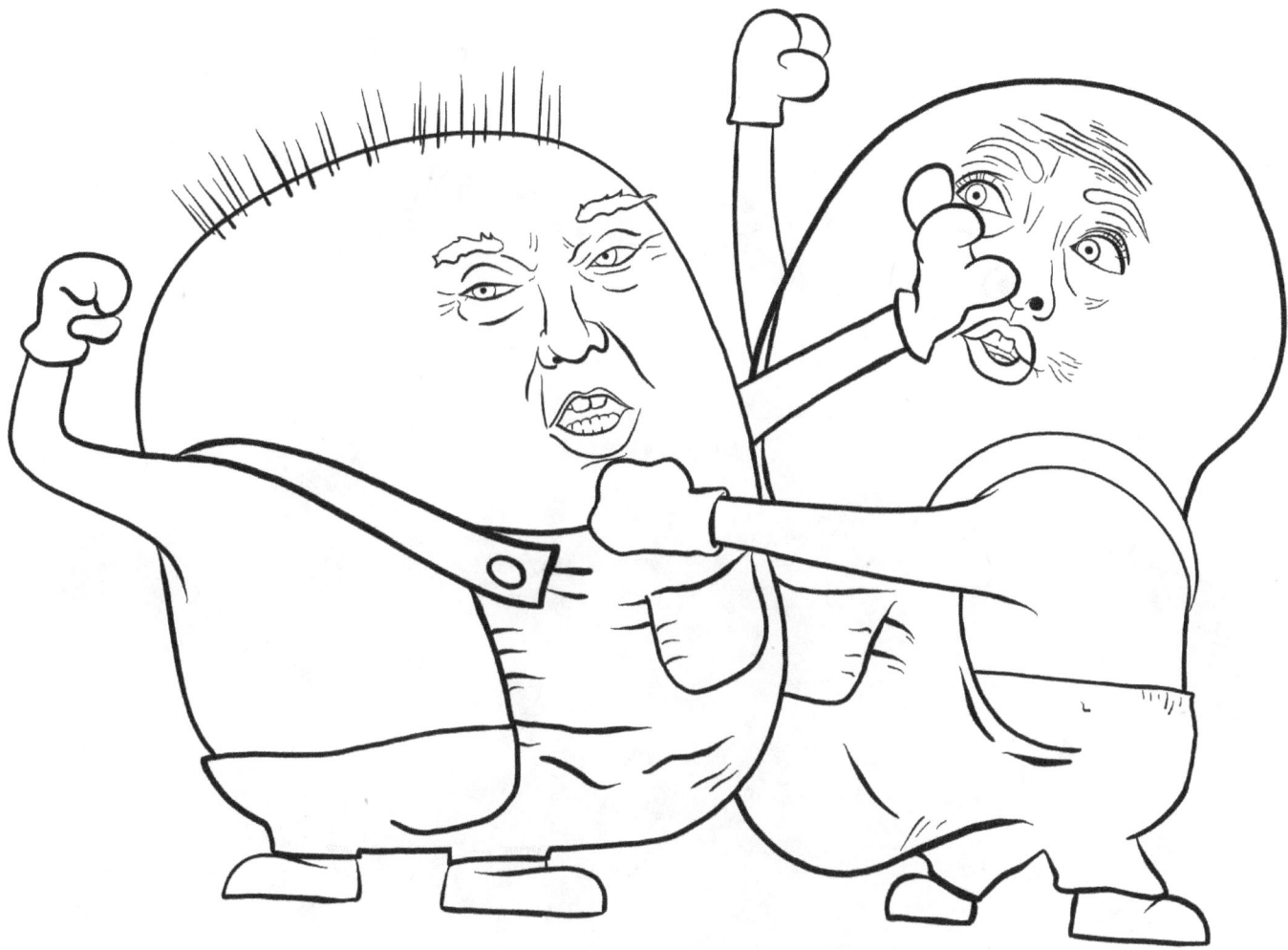

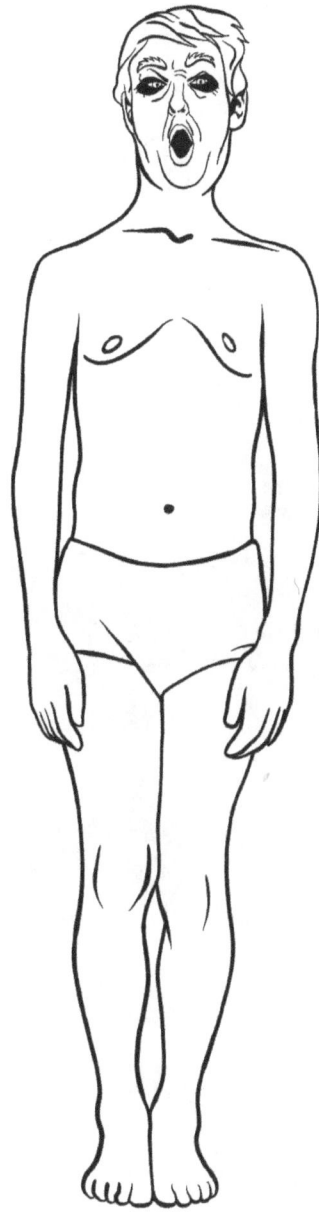

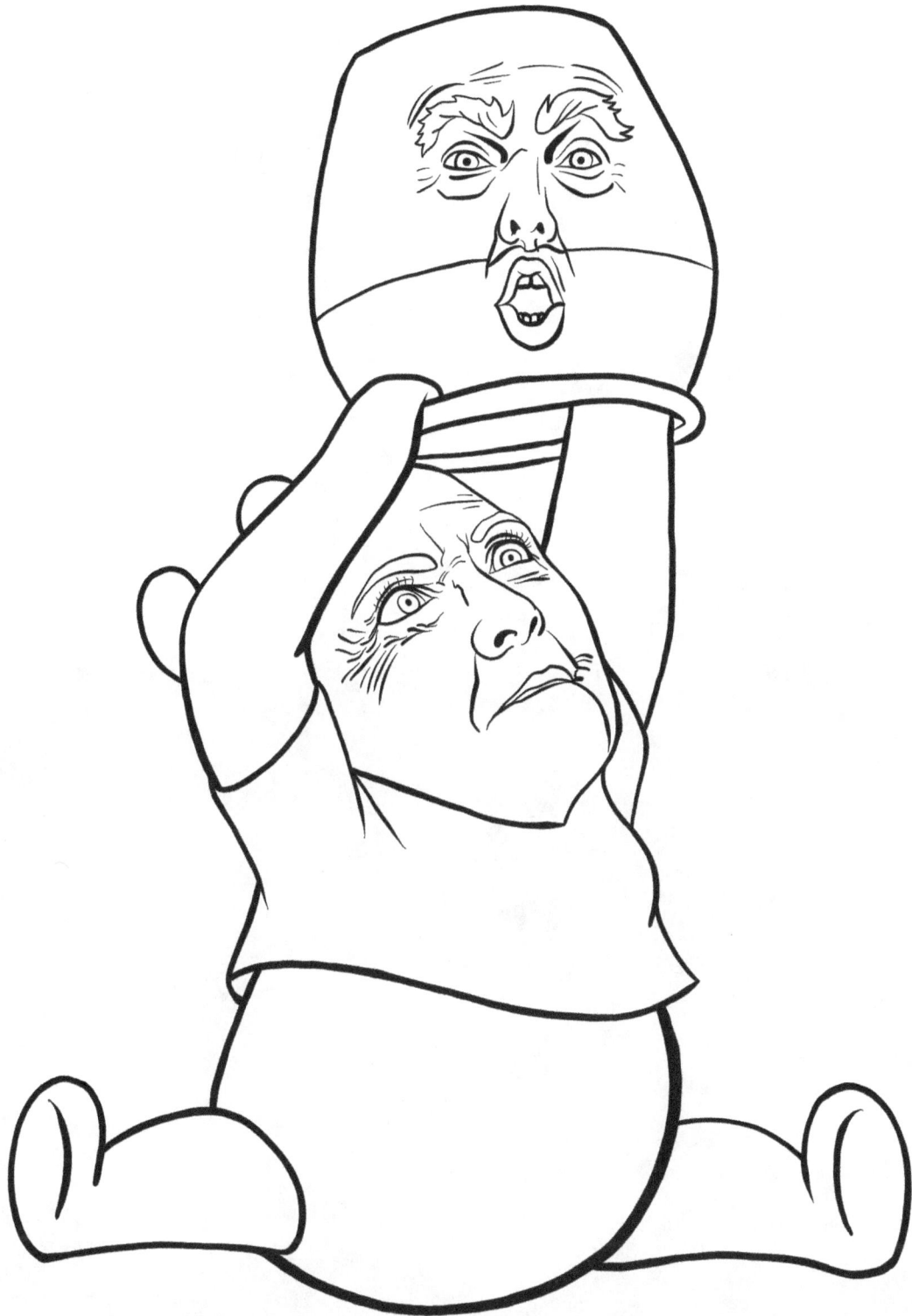

CHECK OUT MORE COLORING BOOKS!

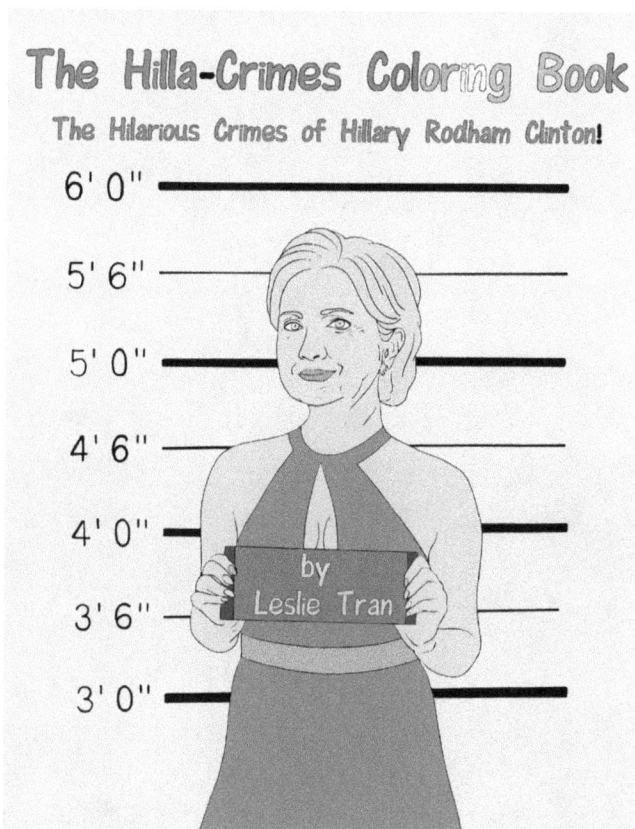

The Hilla-Crimes Coloring Book: The Hilarious Crimes of Hillary Rodham Clinton!

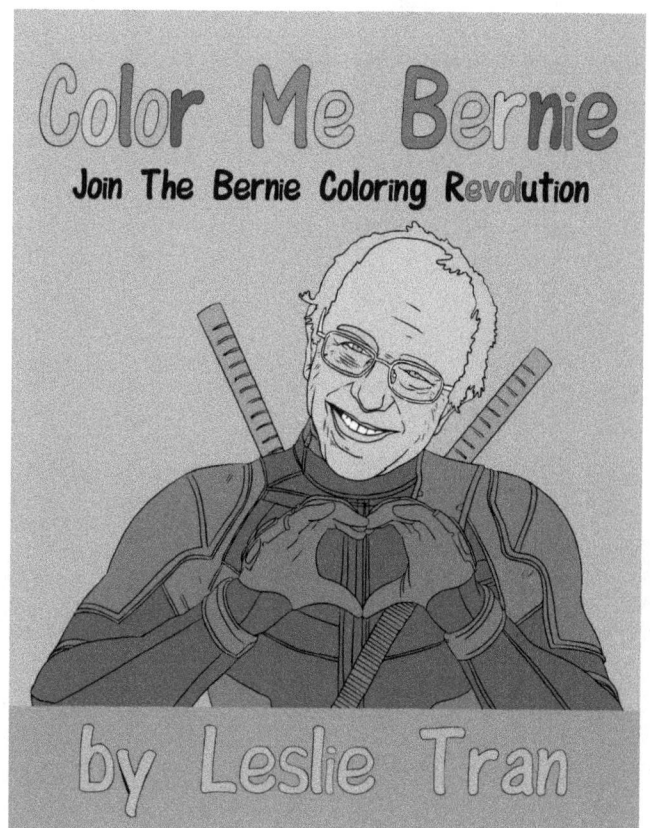

Color Me Bernie: Join The Bernie Coloring Revolution

AVAILABLE ON
AMAZON AND BARNES AND NOBLE